Claim Victory Over Your Scars

Written By
Karen Kutassy

LLCN: <u>2025925121</u>

Copyright Content © 2025

Prologue
CLAIM VICTORY OVER YOUR SCARS

Vision

My vision for this book is to free your soul of all negativity and emotional/physical baggage that has burdened you in your life and to let go of the old way of thinking about yourself and the trauma you have been through. The goal is for you to regain your true self without hiding your imperfections. It is designed to give you freedom and encouragement by dealing with your scars, whether they are physical or emotional. You are worthy and deserving of regaining control over your life. Included in this reading are tools that you can use at any time of the day or night to remove the stigma that your scars are to remain a burden. My wish for you is to reveal your story to the people you love to free yourself of the challenge of keeping it hidden and secret. You can expose the challenges of life to liberate them from your innermost being. Relief will be accomplished when you embark on this journey of letting go and starting anew.

If you have been mistreated unfairly, abused, betrayed, neglected, abandoned, or humiliated, this book was made for you. You will be given facts about how life can be unfair and strategies on how to receive help in the healing process to work through it. You will learn how to gain strength and resilience to deal with your past abuse and to move into the future as a happy, whole person.

Becoming whole again will give you the freedom you need to be a productive, confident, and wholesome individual.

About the Author

Karen Kutassy grew up in a happy nurturing home that shaped her belief in the power of perseverance, resilience, confidence, and strength. But life's challenges later tested those very qualities and through her own journey of healing, she discovered how inner scars can become sources of growth, not defeat. Her messages are heartfelt and sincere. With warmth and honesty, she reminds readers that even through pain, it is possible to rise stronger, live boldly, and find victory in every scar.

Dedication

This book is dedicated to the female population of all ages, race, ethnicity, and religion worldwide.

Empower yourselves, set goals, and strive to reach them.

Acknowledgement

This book was written after I was inspired by Pastor Steve Bilsborough of Great Life Church in Brooksville Florida sermon on scars. My negative assumptions on this topic were changed to a positive thought process.

Claiming victory over your scars will set you free.

I want to acknowledge Joe Clark and the team from Book Writing Website in finalizing this book. Their advice, creative ideas, and expertise on publishing and marketing was priceless.

Introduction

I was inspired to write this book after I attended Great Life Church in Brooksville, Florida and Pastor Steve Bilsborough preached on the topic of 'SCARS.' The information was so profound that I knew I had to expand on the knowledge I received since I have never perceived scars as a victory. The Pastor's words helped me see scars as a positive aspect rather than a negative one. There were words of wisdom preached that Sunday by Pastor Bilsborough, which turned my thought processes into a better understanding of how our natural behavior would be to hide our physical scars because they aren't attractive and can be disfiguring. I am among the population that prefers to avoid showing my negative side or any scars on my skin. I recently had a minor procedure on my face. I found the residual mark to be unsightly and perceived the site as larger than it was. My only option was to apply Vaseline and to cover it with a band aid because those were the doctor's orders. I was appreciative that it had to be covered for about two weeks until it healed. I also tend to internalize any major conflicts I may be having with another person instead of hashing it out. Thanks for your hard work attempt to solve the conflict. Reminiscing about negative experiences, be it a physical altercation, verbal outburst, or any other event that negatively impacted you, is not a pleasant experience. If you strive to be a whole person again, it is necessary to get past the hurt and pain with the help and guidance from people that have experienced similar events or through putting your trust in a friend, relative, clergy, or a therapist. First and foremost, you need to get to the point in your life where you are accepting the fact that this event occurred. It happened; now you are responsible to act in your favor to form a plan of action to prevent it from happening again. This is easier said than done, but with guidance, determination, and perseverance, you can improve your life. The alternate option would be to harbor it within you for the rest of your life or to continue to let the abuse happen. Think about the following questions carefully. Which option do you think is healthier for you? Which option do you think would be more difficult to solve? Working through it or living with it?

Abuse can cause constrictions, low self-esteem, a lack of confidence, and the inability to move on with your life. Have you been carrying a sack of invisible rocks on your shoulders and walking with your head down, moving throughout your daily routine of work and responsibilities? Is it like walking on eggshells in your home or when you are around a certain person? Do you have an occasional flashback of the event or events, or are you burdened constantly with the memories of the injustice done to you? Read on, and you will gain the insight that will help you in your exploration to a better self.

We have all suffered in one way or another during our time on this earth, and we all have a story to tell. This book aims to liberate you from your emotional or physical scars, empowering you to progress on your life's path.

Chapter 3 includes Christian beliefs on this subject and gives insight on the positive way in which humans can manage imperfections. God did not make us perfect because he knew that we would sin and have strife in our lives. The only perfect one is God, and he is always divinely present for you to talk to and guide you.

"People look at the outward appearance, but the Lord looks at the heart."
-1 Samuel 16:7-

Table of Contents

Prologue 3

About the Author 6

Dedication 7

Acknowledgement 8

Introduction 9

Chapter 1 16

- Definitions and synonyms used in this book

Chapter 2 17

- Emotional Scars and their effect on you
- Bad things happen to good people
- Trust shattered
- Verbal Abuse
- Depression/Anxiety
- I am not good enough
- Words spoken that hurt
- Fear of reporting the abuser
- Isolation

Chapter 3 20

- Physical Scars
- Types of Scars
- Scars compared to wrinkles
- Covering up scars and marks
- Free yourself from bondage
- You deserve to be loved
- Dealing with unpleasant memories

Chapter 4 22

- Alleluia! Help the Christian Way
- See it, Feel it, Deal with it
- You've been healed
- The battle was won
- Scars as a teaching tool
- Reveal your scar
- You are victorious
- Allow God to guide you
- Stand Mighty and Strong

Chapter 5 24

- Strategies on How to Recover
- Form a support system
- A shoulder to cry on
- Let your guard down
- Reminiscence on Happier Times
- Never Give up
- Purge out negativity
- Tell your story
- Strength and confidence
- Meditation
- Pet Therapy
- Journaling
- Relive the event
- Accept your true self

Chapter 6 28

- True Stories
- The Authors Story

- Dont ever give up
- The Homeless Man
- Becky's Story
- Childhood trauma
- I won't take it anymore

Chapter 7 35

- Be a Friend, not a Judge
- Be supportive
- Use your listening skills
- Silence can be Golden
- Offer to do chores and errands
- Avoid drama
- Plan a short outing
- Form a team
- Encourage professional help
- Suggest positive affirmations
- Maintain Confidentiality

References 38

Chapter 1

Definitions & Synonyms Used in this Book

1.*Intimidation:* To threaten, deter or to frighten: arm twisting, terrifying, scaring, unnerving, threatening, domineering, browbeating, coercion, harassment.

2.*Rejection*: Being turned down and dismissed: suppression, ban, castaway, no, declining.

3. *Betrayed:* Being harmed by the intentional actions of a trusted person to lead astray, to fail in a time of need, to deceive: treachery, disloyal, double cross.

4.*Injustice:* Lack of fairness, an unjust act; abuse, unlawful, dishonesty.

5.*Neglect*: Fair to care for properly; fail to care for, abandon, leave alone, ignore.

6.*Verbal Abuse*: Hurting others by silence or with words as a weapon; insult, reprimand, verbal attack, slander, vilification, character of assassination.

7.*Physical Abuse:* Intentional harm to the body; injury: being cowed, browbeaten, tormented, worked over, sandbagged.

Chapter 2

Emotional Scars and its Effect on Us

The definition of emotional scars is a feeling of great emotional pain or sadness that is caused by a bad experience and can last for a long time.

When someone wrongs us and causes hurt and pain, our natural reaction is to question whether we did anything to trigger the event. It's easy to put the blame on ourselves. We are human beings that want to be loved and not hurt. Unfortunately, bad things happen to good people. Our emotions can operate on a scale ranging from euphoria to depression, depending on how our lives proceed and how we are treated by the people we are associated with. When we are betrayed, it shatters the trust we may have felt for that person or people. Each person's strife and pain are their own, but what is done with it is imperative and depends on our survival.

Chronic verbal abuse and intimidation that hurts a person's feelings are far more damaging to our general well-being and to our psyche than other types of abuse. Emotional trauma can affect the way a person copes in a healthy way because it distorts the thought processes. Feelings of helplessness, hopelessness, depression, and suicidal ideation are common in a percentage of people that have been treated in an unjust manner. Words spoken that make us feel rejected, demeaned, intimidated, or ridiculed can provoke anxiety and depression. These words damage our ego and cause deeper pain as they impact our self-esteem and confidence. We may not feel that we are good enough to have friends, socialize, or seek employment.

Emotional scars do not heal as much as a scar on our skin does. Instead, the hurt and pain settle down deep in our core, warm and comfortable for years or for the rest of our lives.

During years of growing up, our parents, siblings, uncles, aunts, and other family members may have cut us down so low with their words that we don't feel like we are a whole person. Their intentions may be to truly hurt or be unintentional. Humans of all ages are hurting emotionally but are too frightened to speak up or ask for help. Fear of reporting the person who is neglecting or abusive plays a major role in not seeking the help that is needed. Stress, hardship and lack of having the skills to deal with the abuse can weigh us down and steal our joy and well-being. If you have been the victim of emotional or other abuse, the confidence you may have had at one time has lessened or is nonexistent, leading to feelings of desperation, inferiority, and shyness. These negative emotions may give the idea that no one can help you. This mindset is dangerous and non-productive.

An emotionally scarred person may fold into themselves like a turtle who recedes into its shell for protection. This self-protection allows a feeling of safety, enforcing a chance to self-reflect and to formulate a plan on how to improve their situation.

It may also cause further isolation and desperation.

Every person's strife and pain are their own, but what is done about it is imperative and depends on survival.

The Lord is close to the brokenhearted and saves those who are crushed in spirit.
--Psalm 34:18—

Chapter 3

Physical Scars

Among many other factors, a healed surgical incision, an accident, self-inflicted, an animal bite, carelessness, or abuse, can all result in physical scars on our bodies. In a way, scars can be compared to wrinkles on the skin. Wrinkles are visible and cannot be fully hidden. Mars, scars, and wrinkles are part of us at some point in life. Each crease or line, whether deep or superficial, tells a story. The deeper the lines, the more stories you can share. You have been through a hurtful event and survived. The finer lines are signs that you are just getting started. Life has yet to throw you the curveballs that may occur throughout your lifetime. As vain human beings, we naturally seek to conceal physical scars, marks, or abnormalities through clothing, make-up, creams, dermatology procedures, or home remedies. Our goals should be to strive to open ourselves up to the world and free ourselves by sharing our story with others. We must be unchained from the bondage we are in, then look in the mirror at ourselves to reveal who we are. We are all as lovely as God made us. Humans deserve to be loved, and they deserve to give love back in the purest of ways. Scars are part of us, but we can't let it prevent us from getting our groove back and being an active part of society.

Pastor Bilsborough preached that, "hiding scars gives us a false sense of reality of who we are. You don't want to be reminded of the scars of the past." 1 Some of us prefer to keep the past buried deep within our soul allowing it to remain there for a lifetime because it is too painful to analyze in-order-to move on to a better psychological understanding. To dwell on the scars we have, whether it be emotional or physical, reminds us that we went through it. We were in the battle and unpleasant memories are not to be forgotten. Do we bury them or deal with them? Ponder on these questions, then come up with a solid answer, then act on it.

A happy heart makes the cheerful, but
heartache crushes the spirit.
--Proverbs 15:13--

Chapter 4

Alleluia! Help the Christian Way

A quote from Pastor Bilsborough states, "God never said it hurt when he was suffering on the cross because he wanted to please his Heavenly Father."2 Christians view scars as divine signs from God, not as evidence of pain, signifying your healing. "Some of the most anointed people come from the hood." 3 They have seen it, felt it, dealt with it, and they conquered the trenches and survived adversity. "You didn't run away and stayed in the battle. Your scars are the memorial of the battles you had to win." 4 The anointed individual can utilize their scars to their advantage and impart their wisdom to as many listeners as possible. Think of your scars and reveal them as a teaching tool to help others see that with Jesus's guidance you will come out victorious. We are the head and not the tail. The wisdom gained can help the weak and hurt if you kneel and pray with them. Aid them in comprehending that there is no need to be phony and scars do not have to remain hidden and a secret. There is no need to stress over wearing long sleeves, cake make-up on our faces, and spending money on scar removal procedures. Let God set you free of your hiding. "God is not searching out perfect human beings because he is searching for the weak and he wants them to own their scars." 5

God knows we can conquer the negative events in our lives. We can rise above our self-consciousness with his spiritual guidance. God can qualify you as a victorious person who will overcome your hurts by not hiding behind a mask. Restore joy and happiness by being true to God first, then to yourself and others. Pastor Steve preached, "Your scars will always be a part of you, but you will claim victory over them. Claim them as your trophy." 6 You will regain your complete identity, both internally and externally. You can tell a story about what you endured and how you made it through your journey. Now you can stand mighty and strong with Jesus guiding you every step of the way. Do not let the past define who you are now in your life.

The Lord is close to the brokenhearted and saves those who are crushed in spirit.
--Psalm 43:18--

Chapter 5

Strategies on How to Recover

Managing the trauma experienced is imperative for quality of life over a lifetime. It is important that you do not go through the recovery process alone. Instinctively, it will be known when to begin. You need the unconditional and judgement-free support of a trusted family member, friend, teacher, social worker, co-worker, clergy, therapist, or anyone else during this time. It's important to know where you want to be and how you want to feel. A support system is to be put in place to have someone to lean on, a shoulder to cry on, and to verbalize and share thoughts and feelings. This may be a difficult task, but for healing, letting your guard down and allowing yourself to be vulnerable is the key. Giving permission to use the support system as a lifeline will get you through the tough times. Experience the journey of regaining self-respect, dignity, and confidence with an open mind. Remember the times when you were a shining star and happy. Strive to feel like that again and reach that level of self-satisfaction and contentment. By committing to work at it, you will become the person you want to be. Never give up the fight to get your SWAG back.

In the following strategies, when our thoughts bring us to what we have gone through, we can allow ourselves to be in the moment and express those emotions through crying, angry shoutouts, punching a pillow, taking a hike through the woods, swimming in the ocean, or stomping our feet on the floor. We can allow ourselves to feel the fear by letting our body shake or meditate to purge out the negativity. Having a trusted friend or partner with us for support is necessary. Simply and calmly tell a partner or loved one how the scars were obtained. By revealing the story, it may help the loved one reveal events they may have experienced but have kept a secret. They may be set free because secrets were shared. In helping others, you will regain confidence and strength. In readings from the self-help book: Meditations on Self Love, written by Laurasia Mattingly, it reads, "You will make it through. Be brave to show others they can do it too. Reveal yourself and by opening up to others, it will be monumental in self-healing and reflection." Another way to help heal is by imagining, that one part and another part of the psyche is in the present where it is safe. Through meditation, we can allow the effects of past events to dissipate, recognizing that they no longer reside within us and that we are now safe.

An organization called ESA: Emotional Support Animal Group has been monumental in training animals to provide support and love for persons diagnosed with emotional conditions. The animal is trained to sense when an episode is about to happen. It will perform his specific action to help the person feel secure and loved.

Journals are a cathartic way to express our life story and daily emotions, including the good times and the bad. If we are unable to verbally express how we feel, putting it into words can help heal your soul. Writing entries in a journal can help solve the dilemma because it can be read as many times as needed. Kristin Neff, PhD, explains in her book Fierce Self-Compassion that you can utilize a method of compassionate letter writing by journaling the traumatic experience, attempting to recall the physical sensations or emotions associated with the event. Then think of how you will not accept being humiliated anymore. As you are recalling what happened, write ways that you can treat yourself with gentleness. The concept is that you can train yourself in self-comfort strategies to help you recover or deal with current emotional trauma or setbacks. To heal, you must allow yourself to feel the emotions. Dr. Neff recommends that after you write down the painful event, you must allow yourself to feel the anger and form a plan on how to use it constructively. Ask yourself, can you do anything to prevent it from occurring again? Share your experience and knowledge with others? By sharing, you will also work through your own dilemma. The way out of our cage begins with accepting absolutely everything about ourselves and our lives by embracing with care our moment-to-moment experiences.

It is natural to develop a negative attitude in life if you have been treated with injustice repeatedly. Dr. Eva Selhub, MD explains in her novel titled, "Resilience for dummies," That if you have developed a cynical outlook on life, it would be helpful if you observe yourself and how often you use negative statements and how do it affect your demeanor."

A therapist would be a good resource to help analyze your behavior.

We all have a different way of processing and filtering out information. Working with a therapist will help you develop the strategy that best suits you to work on your emotional pain.

In the novel Better Than Ever, written by April Osteen Simons, she urges us to take our zeal for life back. "Repossess your hope. Plant that smiles back on your beautiful face. Get your happiness back! When you wake up every morning, sit up and tell the world. "I have a reason for getting out of bed! I'm excited for this day."

> ***Therefore. If anyone is in Christ, the new creation has come: The old has gone, the new is here!***
> --2 Corinthians 5:17—

Chapter 6

True Stories
Story One: My Story

Reflecting on my life, it has primarily been a fulfilling journey, albeit marked by occasional challenges. The highlight of my life was being a parent of two children, who I am so proud of in all realms. I experienced the same ups and downs that I feel most people go through, which include happiness, fulfillment, accomplishments in my education and career, and feeling that I was a fair and solid parent. I also had negative occurrences, which over the years have taught me resilience, perseverance, and to always get back up after you have fallen. It was a steppingstone that has given me the emotional stability, confidence, and strength I have now. I have been the victim of verbal and physical abuse on a milder scale than other people. About every 5 years, I would receive an unexpected punch in the arm. Every time it happened in my 35 years of marriage, I was shocked, and I did not react and did not have the skills to know how to deal with it. I would sit quietly as if in a trance without thinking or questioning, why did that happen?

The last straw was when we were going away for the weekend and we were driving over a bridge when he punched me on the side of my face after I ended a conversation with my niece. I retaliated by hitting him back for the first and last time, which resulted in his glasses falling off. He calmly said, "I don't want you talking to her."

Again, it happened without warning, and we obviously had a ruined weekend.

I understand the devastation a person feels when you think all is well and then, BOOM, you get punched like a snake strikes its victim swiftly and quietly. The question that crosses your mind is, "Why did that happen when there was no provocation?" There were happy times intermingled with uncertain and unhappy times. I kept riding the waves as they came and found it easier to not deal with the deeper issues because it took too much energy, and I didn't want to acknowledge that a problem existed. I suffered the difficult times in silence because I didn't want anyone to know that our marriage was not a perfect one. It would have been embarrassing to acknowledge openly that my life was not as perfect as everyone else saw it. My children never witnessed any of my abuse, and it was never talked about. After 35 years of marriage, I divorced because I was truly unhappy for years, and I became afraid of his sporadic anger. In retrospect, the most important lesson learned was to never suffer alone. Swallow your pride and embarrassment and seek help from family members, trusted friends, or a professional. These are times where support and advice are needed. With the abundance of resources available, there is no reason to deal with abuse alone. I encourage anyone enduring negative life issues to reach out and verbalize the issue to a trusted person. Dealing with this confusing time is crucial, as failing to do so can result in years of uncertainty and discernment. The phrase, "walking on eggshells comes to mind."

Why walk on eggshells when you can have solid footing? Seek out help for reassurance, guidance, and support. My advice is for any person in an abusive situation to always have what I call a "Plan B." Confide in a friend and give her a code that can be texted or spoken over the phone to alert her that you are unsafe and you need help. Devise a plan together and ask if you can stay with her when you need a safe place. Have the emergency app on your phone to dial 911 is a good strategy to have in place, and video any events for proof if you can. Go to the police station and ask about a restraining order. You must decide and stick to it, so the abuser knows that you are not going to take it anymore. Establish the mindset; it stops here and right now. I will not be a victim anymore, and getting angry will fuel your determination to take action to keep you safe. The most important part of this story is that I have forgiven him, and I am not carrying a sack of rocks on my shoulders for the rest of my life. If he ever needed my assistance, I would lend a hand and feel good about it.

My profession is a registered nurse with 45 years of experience. I will never forget one case for the rest of my life. A family member found a neglected woman in the basement. She was malnourished and had wounds. No one knew her whole history because she did not speak. She would not make eye contact, show expression, or attempt to interact in any way. She was shut down emotionally. Day after day, month after month, the other nurses and I cared for her needs until her health permitted her transfer to another facility. On the final day, I gave her a popsicle, and when I placed it in her hands, she showed a hint of emotion and a smile, thoroughly enjoying and savoring it. Despite her untold story and the obvious physical wounds, we treated, this was the most mysterious and rewarding case of my entire career. We received her as a broken and frightened human being who was not able to tell us her story. Even though her circumstances will never be known, there is always a glimmer of hope in any situation. That hint of a smile reassured me that she is coming out of her trauma ever so slowly with the help of nurses giving her the tender, loving care she desperately needed. This example illustrates that our bodies and souls can endure unbearable times, but there is hope and we should never give up the fight.

EVER!!!

Gather up all of the will and strength you have left to find hope when you feel hopeless, find strength when you feel weak, speak up when you can't speak, and remember that you are a deserving human being living on this earth and you have the right to live a happy and fulfilling life. Take it. You own it. It is yours to have. Grab life up and hold onto it with all your strength and might. Be victorious and delete the victim mentality from your thoughts. Expect, and make it a requirement, that you receive love, acceptance, respect, and sincerity in your relationships. Do not just settle with anyone, and you will find peace and happiness.

Story Two: A Homeless Man Encounter

Recently, I had the pleasure of meeting a twenty-six-year-old homeless man who was sitting on a curb, playing his ukelele with his worn-out backpack. The ukelele piqued my interest, prompting me to stop and inquire if he needed any assistance. Since I am a beginner in playing the ukelele, he let me play his for a little while. In my short interlude with him, I gained insight one-on-one into how he lived in foster homes all his life. He said he has been hurt and had a rough life. He shared that during his vulnerable moments as an adult, his way of dealing with his turmoil from the past is to allow himself to feel what it was like at the time. He said that giving himself permission to feel the emotions and circumstances associated with it helps him have closure and feel forgiveness. He has mood swings stemming from his past demons. His motto in life is to treat people with kindness, not malice. I discovered that money holds no significance for him, as he relies on numerous resources for his survival, such as dumpster diving for food and clothing, sleeping during the day to conserve energy and prevent dehydration, and relying on hitchhiking for transportation. This young man has been through it and will most likely deal with his past events for the rest of his life, but he is resilient and may help other people in his situation someday.

Story Three: Becky Gobles Story

Becky Goble is a friend of mine who describes her childhood and that she was physically abused daily. As a child, she didn't have any resources to seek help, but at one point in her adult life, she stood up to her mother because she was not going to be a victim anymore. As a preteen, her mother openly told her that she was not planned or wanted, and she attempted to abort her several times during the pregnancy. Her mother also told Becky that she would never succeed in life, as her efforts would never meet expectations. This abuse resulted in extreme shyness, introversion, and low self-esteem, and a constant fear of not being liked by others. Becky remembers thinking that she was ugly and used to walk with her head down. Her other siblings would not get any abuse. At one point in adulthood, she had the urge to hit her mother back, which she did not do. At 19, she began individual therapy to address her insecurities and received exercises to express her emotions during conflicts. She does not have any grudges against her mother and has forgiven her. She currently does not tolerate any form of mistreatment. She speaks her mind and has learned to treat people with fairness. Today, she is a self-assured person who has had a successful career and a stable life. Instead of enduring this issue in silence, she sought help, gaining confidence, speaking her mind, and refusing to tolerate any form of abuse. Her entire childhood and adulthood were filled with abuse.

She is a success story and has used her wisdom to educate whoever may come her way that needs a listening ear and support.

But God will never forget the needy; the hope of the afflicted will never perish.
—Psalm 9:10—

Chapter 07

Be A Friend, not a Judge

This final chapter aims to provide guidance to you, as a trusted friend, therapist, clergy or relative on how to approach a victim in a compassionate and non-judgmental way.

1: Please do not ridicule or lecture. The victim does not need to feel that they are doing something wrong.

2. Be positive and supportive

3. Do not be negative and scorning

4. Give them a listening ear and a shoulder to cry on. There is no need to say anything sometimes but, "I'm sorry!" Silence can be goldened at times.

5. Ask, "What can I do to help you? I'm here for you."

6. Do not react to their story in a dramatic way. Stay neutral and empathetic.

7. If they are unable to express their story then just be there. Your presence is reassuring.

8. Offer to cook them dinner or do the laundry or dishes.

9. Pampering is what they may need. Paint their fingernails,

give a foot massage, or massage the neck and shoulders.

10. Go together to a beach or the mountains and pack a lunch.

11. Recommend that counseling may be helpful.

12. Teaming up with another trusted (safe) person could be effective.

13. If the victim does not want to be alone then pack an overnight bag and stay if possible.

14. Research trauma hotlines in the area and put the numbers on their refrigerator.

15. Suggest that they see their physician to order anti-anxiety medication.

16. If the victim is up to it go shopping then have lunch out.

17. Be in the moment and do not pour out your own troubles.

18. Pray out loud if they are receptive.

19. You can privately pray for them on your own time.

20. Be their "**ROCK**."

21. Tell them that they are a good person and loved and good things will be coming.

22. Accompany them to the police station if a report must be made. They will need you.

23. To maintain trust, keep the conversations confidential.

"Community means that people come together around the table, not just to feed their bodies, but to feed their minds and their relationships."
- Henri J.M. Nouwen –

References

1. Bilsborough, S, "Scars", Great Life Church, Brooksville, Fl, July 24th, 2024

2. Https://freerepublic.com/tag/pray/index?=12752259.

3. Mattingly, L (2020), Meditation on Self-Love, Rockridge Press

4. Neff, K, PhD, (2020), Fierce Self-Compassion. How woman can harness Kindness to Speak Up, Claim Their Power, and Thrive, For Dummies.

5. Simons, Osteen, A (2021), Better Than Ever, Post Hill Press

6. Selhub, E, PhD, (2021), Resilience for Dummies, For Dummies.

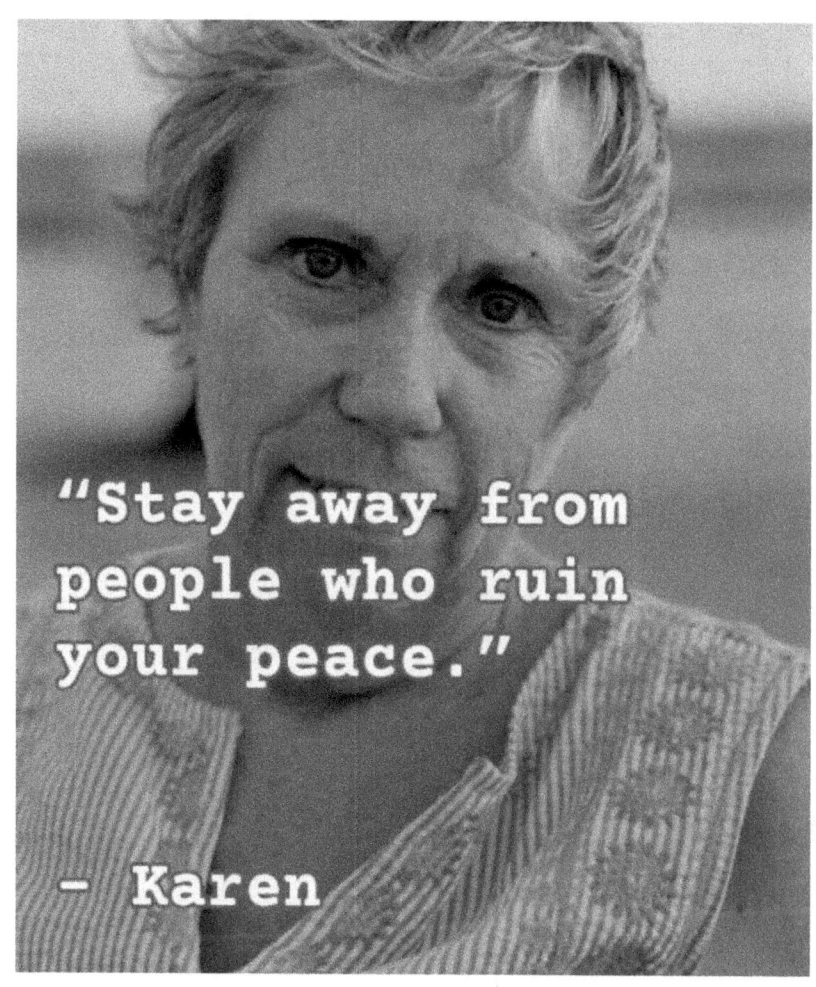

Thankyou!

www.ingramcontent.com/pod-product-compliance
Lightning Source LLC
Chambersburg PA
CBHW061311040426
42444CB00010B/2596